www.raintreepublishers.co.uk
Visit our website to find out
more information about
Raintree books.

To order:

☎ Phone 0845 6044371

▤ Fax +44 (0) 1865 312263

✉ Email myorders@raintreepublishers.co.uk

Customers from outside the UK please telephone +44 1865 312262

Raintree is an imprint of Capstone Global Library Limited,
a company incorporated in England and Wales having its
registered office at 7 Pilgrim Street, London, EC4V 6LB
– Registered company number: 6695582

Edited by Daniel Nunn, Rebecca Rissman, and Sian Smith
Designed by Joanna Hinton-Malivoire
Picture research by Mica Brancic
Production by Victoria Fitzgerald
Originated by Capstone Global Library Ltd
Printed and bound in China by Leo Paper Products Ltd

ISBN 978 1 406 22437 5 (hardback)
15 14 13 12 11
10 9 8 7 6 5 4 3 2 1

ISBN 978 1 406 22444 3 (paperback)
16 15 14 13 12
10 9 8 7 6 5 4 3 2 1

British Library Cataloguing in Publication Data
Nunn, Daniel.
    Voices. -- (Instruments and music)
    1. Singing--Juvenile literature.
    I. Title II. Series
    783-dc22

Acknowledgements
We would like to thank the following for permission to reproduce
photographs: Getty Images pp. 7 (Redferns/Odile Noel), 12
(Hans-Martin Issler), 18 (for the Tribeca Film Festival/Roger Kisby);
Photolibrary pp. 4 (Corbis), 8 (Janine Wiedel), 9 (LOOK-foto/Ulla
Lohmann), 10 (Radius Images), 14 (Ingram Publishing RF), 15 (White/
John Molloy), 17 (Westend61/Hans Huber), 21 (Radius Images), 22
(All Canada Photos/Glenn Bartley), 23 top (Ingram Publishing RF),
23 middle top (Moodboard Moodboard), 23 middle bottom (Glow
Images, Inc.), 23 bottom (White/John Molloy); Shutterstock pp. 5 (©
Jason Stitt), 6 (© Dmitriy Shironosov), 11 (© Jack.Qi), 13 (© Dmitriy
Shironosov), 16 (© withGod), 19 (© Andreas Gradin), 20 (© Anton
Gvozdikov).

Cover photograph of villagers performing a traditional song and
dance in Malawi, reproduced with permission of Getty Images (The
Image Bank/Simon Rawles). Back cover photograph of a gospel choir
reproduced with permission of Photolibrary (Radius Images).

We would like to thank Jenny Johnson, Nancy Harris, Dee Reid, and
Diana Bentley for their assistance in the preparation of this book.

Contents

Musical instruments

saxophone

guitar

People play many instruments to make music.

Some people use their voices to make music. This is called singing.

Singing

Some people sing along with other musical instruments.

Some people sing without any musical instruments.

Some people sing inside.

Some people sing outside.

Some people sing with other people.

Some people sing alone.

Opera singers can sing very loudly.

microphone

Pop singers use microphones to sound louder.

Humming and whistling

Not all singing has words. You can hum a tune with your mouth closed.

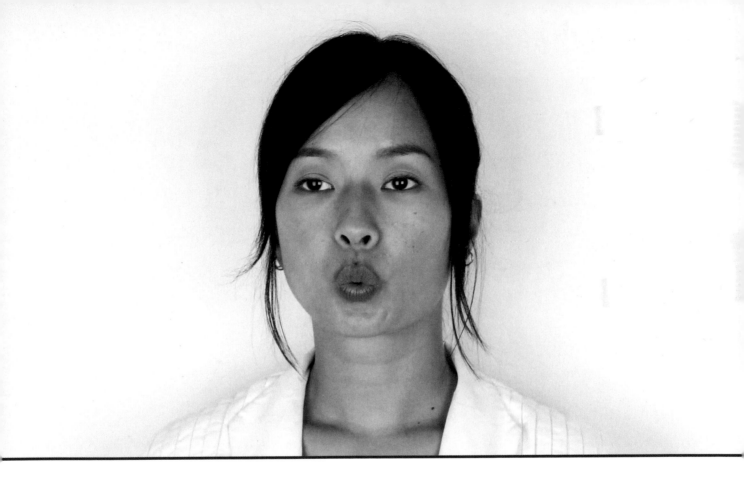

You can whistle a tune by blowing through your teeth and lips.

Unusual voices

Throat singers sing using their throats.

Yodellers sing low notes and high notes all in one breath.

Beatboxers use their voices to make the sounds of drums.

Rappers speak songs instead of singing them.

Why do people sing?

Some people sing for work.

Some people sing for fun!

Birdsong

People are not the only animals that sing. Some birds can sing many

different songs!

Picture glossary

 **hum** sing or make music with your lips closed

 **microphone** something you sing into to make your voice louder

 **note** sound made by your voice or another musical instrument

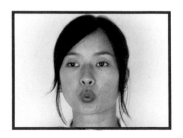 **whistle** make a musical sound by blowing through your teeth and lips

Index

Notes for parents and teachers

Before reading
Explain that people use their voices for talking, but they also use them for singing. Discuss different types of singing with the children. What different types of singing can they think of? What types of singing do they enjoy?

After reading
Discuss the fact that singing doesn't only mean singing words. Encourage the children to try to make different sounds with their voices. Ask them to try singing in a high voice, a low voice, a quiet voice, a loud voice, and so on. Can they recognize when people are singing in a high voice or a low voice?

Extra information
People have vocal folds, which are used for talking, singing, laughing, crying, and so on. There are three parts: the lungs, which produce air and make the air vibrate through the vocal folds (like a woodwind instrument); the larynx, which changes the length of the folds to make the sound higher or lower (like a brass instrument); and the mouth, which changes the sound to make it louder or quieter. Men have lower voices than women and children because their vocal folders are larger. Whistling is different to singing because it does not use the voice. It works in the same sort of way as a wind instrument. Air is blown through a hole made by the lips.